WHAT IS YOUR PLAN WHEN YOUR HEALTH FAILS?

14 ways to help protect your assets, investments, and relationships from future long-term care costs.

JIM E. SLOAN, CLTC, LTCP

ISBN 978-0-692-19687-8

Book cover design by Cathi Stevenson
www.bookcoverexpress.com

Book cover photo by Kelly Weaver Photography
www.kellyweaverphotography.com

Self-published January 2019

Available in print or for the Kindle at:
www.amazon.com

DISCLAIMER

The discussion of tax laws pertinent to long-term care and long-term care insurance is presented as an educational service to the reader and is intended as part of a general discussion.

The information presented is not all-inclusive, nor is it intended to be. Many of the general rules discussed and examples provided have exceptions and limitations, and as a result, it is possible that the general rule or example may not apply to your particular circumstances.

The content has been based upon the tax laws in effect at the time of publication. Any changes to the tax laws may affect the information presented in this book, including any discussions or examples given.

Jim E. Sloan and LTCi Solutions, LLC does not provide legal, accounting, or tax planning advice. If such advice is needed, the author recommends that you seek the assistance of competent, licensed counsel.

Table of Contents

INTRODUCTION

America is aging. We are living longer than ever before, and over the next 40 years, we will witness the most significant demographic change in U.S. history. The U.S. Census Bureau projects that:[1]

- The 65 and older crowd will grow from about 15% to 17% between 2017-2020, and by 2060, adults age 65 and older, are projected to make up nearly one-quarter of the population. That means one out of every four people in America will be over the age of 65.

- The 85 and older crowd is expected to nearly double by 2035 (from 6.4 million to 11.8 million) and almost triple by 2060 (to 19 million people).

1 www.census.gov, Demographic Turning Points for the United States: Population Projections for 2020 to 2060

We are living longer and longer due to technology, medical science advancements, and medicine.

In my personal life, I've seen my wife's grandfather pass away at the age of 102 of natural causes. I was a pallbearer at my grandmother's funeral after she passed three weeks before her 95th birthday, of natural causes. My wife's grandmother is age 94, and as of the summer of 2018, she is receiving home health care informally by family and enjoys watching Houston Astros and Rockets games on television.

Will everybody live a long life? Of course not, but as you can see by the Bureau's projections, by 2060, one out of every four Americans will be age 65 or above. So how do we plan for living a long life? It starts with having our finances in order.

A big fear of many retirees is outliving their assets. Many retirees are reluctant to tap into their principal, wanting to preserve it at all costs. They want to preserve the income stream but also want to preserve the principal so that they have something to leave to their children, grandchildren, or a favorite charity.

Rarely Discussed Risk

A rarely discussed risk to an investment portfolio is that of an extended care event to one or both retirees. As the likelihood of needing care increases with increased age, the long-term care risk to an investment portfolio becomes larger, not smaller, as we age.

If you were unable to care for yourself, what would you do? Would your spouse be able to care for you? What if your spouse were to pass away before you? What if your spouse was the one who needed care? Would you be able to physically, emotionally, and financially provide the necessary care?

As part of your planning, it's important to acknowledge that living a long life is a near certainty for most of us. And, the longer we live, the more likely we are to need some type of day-to-day assistance.

Medicare, Medicaid, and the Veteran's Administration do not provide for the type of care that we will most likely need, which includes care at home, either informally (family and friends) or formally (paid professionals).

Today, it is possible to design long-term care solutions that will pay informal caregivers (family or friends) that provide care to you.

My Children Will Take Care of Me

I've heard plenty of times that "my children will take care of me". And, they probably will.

Have you walked through that scenario with them?

Does it mean that they will move in with you or will you move in with them and their family?

Does it mean that they will provide hands-on care such as bathing and dressing you?

Or does it mean that they will provide for you financially?

What would the impact be on your adult child's life if they unexpectedly became responsible for your care 24 hours every day for months or years?

What would the consequences be, if they provided care only eight hours a day?

What would that do to their family time? To their career? To their other responsibilities and commitments? What would it mean to them financially?

When a long-term care event happens, it is an event that disrupts not only your life, but everyone else that is in your life.

Inform Your Loved Ones

Inform your loved ones of your care preferences. Have it in writing. Do you want to stay in your current area if you need care or would you move to another part of the country where you have family?

Would you want to move in with your children?

Would you want to receive care at home for as long as possible, or would you prefer to be in a setting such as an Assisted-Living Facility, where there are other aging people around, where there is help as needed, and there are a variety of social activities planned?

If care is needed, how will you pay for it? You have three choices: Medicaid, long-term care insurance or paying out of your pocket.

Some policies will pay for a caregiver to come into your home to provide care for you, informally (family or friends) or formally (professionals).

You can also insure just a portion of your care costs if you feel that you can afford to pay the remaining portion. That's why having a long-term-care planning discussion is so important.

I don't believe everyone needs long-term care insurance, but I strongly believe everyone needs long-term care planning.

Speak to your financial advisor or have him or her contact me if needed, to discuss, design, and implement a plan for the eventuality of needing extended care.

Inform your family of the resources that are available, either in the form of assets or insurance to pay for your care.

Then, enjoy the peace of mind that comes from good planning, and get out there, and enjoy the years that you've been given.

CHAPTER ONE

America, an Aging Nation

Aging is part of the human life cycle, as much as infancy, childhood, adolescence, and adulthood. The aging process is also known as senescence, which begins when we reach adulthood, and is the process of deterioration with age.

The purpose of this chapter is to remind us that if we live the full human life cycle, we will become frail and will need daily assistance from someone at some point in our future. We may need that assistance for many months or years at home before assisted-living or nursing home care becomes a consideration.

To put the human life cycle in perspective as it relates to you and me, ask yourself, "When will I need care?" Let's say it will be 25-30 years from now before you begin needing care. Who else will need that type of care at that time? Millions.

According to a report released by the U.S. Census Bureau in March 2018, the aging population over the next 40 years is going to explode.

Aging Population Explosion[2]

The nation's 65-and-older population is projected to nearly double in size in coming decades, from 49 million today to 95 million people by 2060.

By 2060, older adults are projected to make up nearly 25% of the population. One out of every four people in America will be 65 or older.

The number of people 85 and older is expected to nearly double by 2035 (from 6.4 million to 11.8 million) and nearly triple by 2060 (to 19 million people).

How we prepare physically, emotionally, and financially in our 40's, 50's, and 60's will have a direct impact on the quality of life we'll enjoy in our 70's, 80's, and 90's.

2 U.S. Census Bureau report 'Demographic Turning Points for the United States,' released March 2018

CHAPTER TWO

What is Long-Term Care?

Long-term care, also referred to as extended care, is the time that services and support become necessary to meet health or personal care needs of an individual over an extended period.[3]

The statistics tell us that 70% of all claims for long-term care begin *outside* of a nursing home.[4]

From my perspective as a long-term care planning specialist, the industry (Medicaid and private insurance) have begun to move toward keeping you *out* of a nursing home. Whoever is going to pay your long-term care bills (Medicaid, yourself, or insurance), will want to keep you *out* of a nursing home for as long as possible, because it is the most expensive type of long-term care services today.

3 www.longtermcare.acl.gov
4 2017 LTC Sourcebook, AALTCI

The mutual goal is to have the patient safely stay in their home for as long possible, which most often, is what the patient wants as well.

The government (Medicaid) or insurance companies love this because it saves them a lot of money, giving them an incentive to keep you receiving care at home, a win-win.

Because of this phenomenon, home health care is, and will continue to be the leader in the type of long-term care services provided across the country.

Most Long-Term Care Is Not Health Care

Most long-term care is not medical care, but rather assistance with the necessary tasks of everyday life, which are referred to as Activities of Daily Living (ADLs), such as:

- Bathing
- Dressing
- Using the toilet
- Transferring (to or from bed or chair)

- Caring for incontinence

- Eating

Other common long-term care services and supports are assistance with everyday tasks, sometimes called Instrumental Activities of Daily Living (IADLs) including:

- Housework

- Managing money

- Taking medication

- Preparing and cleaning up after meals

- Shopping for groceries or clothes

- Using the telephone or other communication devices

- Caring for pets

- Responding to emergency alerts such as fire alarms

Long-Term Care is an Event

A long-term care event for you or a family member could completely alter your life as you know it, and the lives of those you love.

If there were not a long-term care plan in place, your loved ones would have no choice but to provide care. For many, life will be radically and irreversibly different from the way it was before the impairment.

The difficult truth is that as impairments worsen, they compromise the person's capacity to interact within their environment safely, which compels others to get involved. The moment extended care is needed, it becomes an event.

Paying the Price

The event causes two sets of irreversible consequences: personal and financial.[5]

Personal consequences refer to the extreme toll the impairment takes on the physical and emotional wellbeing of the caregiver.

5 Harley Gordon's 'The Conversation', 2016

Yes, the impaired person's life is different now, but for unpaid family members providing care, life is completely disrupted.

Thirty-four million Americans are providing unpaid care to loved one's age 50 or older and are paying an incredibly high price in the quality of their own lives as a result.[6]

How many selfless caregivers gave up promotions, took unpaid leave, stopped working altogether, moved back home, and dismantled their lives to provide care for a relative or friend?

A well thought out plan for long-term care would mitigate almost 100% of these issues for you and your family.

6 Caregiving in the United States, AARP report, 2015

CHAPTER THREE

Types of Long-Term Care Services

To determine the type of long-term care services that are needed, a person would display one of two types of impairments: acute or chronic.

Acute impairments require short-term, hospital based medical care, and the patient is expected to recover. However, in the case of a stroke, for instance, an acute medical need could become a chronic condition requiring extended care.

Chronic impairments are ongoing conditions which can be managed but not cured. In the realm of long-term care, chronic impairments are either physical or cognitive.

Physically-impaired people require help with their Activities of Daily Living (ADLs).

Cognitively-impaired people, such as those with Alzheimer's or dementia, have a loss of intellectual capacity, which compromises their ability to get through the day safely.

Two Levels of Care

Depending on the impairment and its severity, there are two levels of care: skilled and custodial.

Skilled care is required to help a person recover from an acute medical event. Skilled care services can only be provided by a physician or under a plan of care created by a physician and executed by a trained nursing staff or other licensed professionals. Inpatient hospitalization or formal rehabilitative services are considered skilled care.

Custodial care is what long-term care is all about. Long-term care requires custodial or non-skilled services, such as physical assistance with Activities of Daily Living or supervision of a cognitively impaired person.

Custodial care is provided either formally by paid professionals or informally by unpaid family and friends with no particular training in health care. It consists of homemaking services, such as cooking and cleaning the house, and direct personal-care assistance to help the person safely get through his or her daily routine.

Informal care is unpaid care given by family members and friends. Most agree that a loved one or close friend would provide care if needed, but an effective long-term care plan with meaningful funding will allow informal caregivers to maintain their own health and lifestyle, while helping those he or she loves.

This doesn't have to be done only from the goodness of their heart, because the right long-term care plan can provide benefits that make money available to pay these informal caregivers. Let me repeat: there are plans today that allow you to pay your family and friends who provide care for you.

Professional custodial care is given by anyone who is paid to provide long-term custodial services in an individual's home or in a special residential community setting. Professional providers of extended-care services can be home-care workers, transportation staff, and those who serve in paid community-based services, such as adult day-care, assisted living, and nursing homes.

CHAPTER FOUR

What Will It Cost for Long-Term Care Services When You Need It?

Let's Talk Costs!

The average cost of long-term care services will vary depending on the region of the country where you live or decide to retire. Since I live in the Denver, Colorado area, I will use that region to illustrate the typical average monthly costs associated with the different types of long-term care services today.

To learn about the costs in the area where you live, google Genworth Cost of Care Survey.

The 2018 average monthly long-term care costs are:

LTC Services Provided	Monthly Cost[7]
Adult Day Care	$1,625
Assisted Living Facility	$4,700
Homemaker Services	$4,767
Home Health Aide	$5,083
Nursing Home (semi-private)	$8,365
Nursing Home (private)	$9,520

To get an accurate portrayal of what long-term care costs will be when you might need care, take the above numbers and increase by 5% annually (for inflation) until you reach age 80. That is the amount of monthly benefits you'll want to solve for. Then, determine how much of that cost you could pay out of pocket and insure the remainder.

7 2017 Genworth Cost of Care Survey

EXAMPLE

Susan is age 60 and lives in Denver. The average monthly cost to live in an Assisted Living Facility today (2018) in the Denver area is $4,700 per month.

Let's further assume Susan won't need extended care until age 80. Now, let's take the monthly $4,700 figure and inflate it at 5% annually for 20 years.

The $4,700/monthly cost today becomes a $12,470/monthly cost when Susan reaches 80.

Said another way, it will cost $149,640 annually after taxes for Susan to enter an Assisted-Living Facility in 20 years.

If Susan needs to enter a nursing home, the number doubles to over $299,280 net annually.

If Susan is married and the unlikely scenario of both needing that level of care, double the numbers again to $598,560 net annually.

As you can see, due to inflation and rising costs in health care, what seems like large long-term care costs today become very large costs as the years go by. You can see that if not planned for, this could disrupt every financial and tax plan you have in place.

That is *one reason* to begin the long-term care conversation in your early 50's to early 60's. The later you wait, the more expensive it becomes.

The *second reason* is that as we age, our bodies start breaking down, so the later you wait, insurability becomes a factor. You'll have to health qualify if your plan includes insurance.

Could you protect your retirement assets and income if you or your spouse, partner, or both, were to need long-term care services for an extended period?

Have you and your financial advisor discussed this topic, so that you have a plan in place the day your health fails? That conversation could be the first step to mitigate the impact that an extended care event could have on your investment and income plan.

Hopefully, this book will become a catalyst for you to take the first step in your long-term care planning, which is to begin that discussion today, and ending with a well thought-out and designed plan of action, so that your family is protected and prepared as possible when that day arrives.

CHAPTER FIVE

Who's Going to Pay for Your Care? Here's 14 Ways!

This chapter addresses 14 insurance and non-insurance ways that consumers utilize to gain access to long-term care coverage. It is designed to give you a basic understanding of each option.

Your personal situation should be discussed with a professional that is knowledgeable in long-term care planning, to help you sort through the detailed information, including the benefits, services offered, exclusions, and costs associated with each option. Only then, can an informed decision be made that's in your best interest.

OPTION #1 – VETERANS ADMINISTRATION

The Veterans Administration (VA) has an underused pension benefit called *Aid and Attendance* that provides money to those who need assistance performing everyday tasks. For veterans and the surviving spouses of veterans who need in-home care or are in a nursing home, help may be available.

Advantages:

- Veterans whose income is above the legal limit for a VA pension may still qualify.

- The veteran does not have to have a service-related disability to qualify.

Disadvantages:

- Veterans must have served at least 90 days, with at least one of those days during wartime.

- To qualify, veterans must meet the income threshold and have less than $80,000 in assets, excluding home and vehicle.

Things to consider:

For veterans that meet the criteria, long-term care services could be covered by the Veterans Administration. Although it is coverage, you will not have the choices as you would, if you were self-pay or insured.

Additional details are available at www.va.gov.

OPTION #2 – FEDERAL LTC INSURANCE PROGRAM

This federal long-term care insurance program is an employer group insurance plan for current and retired federal government employees, including their families.

Advantages:

- More lenient for those with health issues
- Opportunity to secure LTC insurance

Disadvantages:

- Although a group policy, it is not guaranteed-issue
- Married couples tend to pay more

Things to consider:

This insurance program is just one more option to consider amongst others. It's neither good or bad; your personal situation will dictate if it makes sense for you or not.

For additional details on this program, visit www.ltcfeds.com.

OPTION #3 – SELF-INSURE

Self-insuring is an option for those that have significant assets and choose to manage their long-term care risk by funding any future long-term care needs 100% out of their pocket.

Advantages:

- Maintain control of your assets

- No restrictions on how to use your money

- Freedom to choose any care you wish

Disadvantages:

- If you need to sell investments to pay for care in a down market, you may have significant losses.

- If you need to sell investments to pay for care in an up market, you might create a tax liability on the gains, whereas long-term care benefits are income tax-free.

- If long-term care costs escalate and retirement assets shrink, you may risk depleting your retirement savings.

- Your freedom to choose your care may become limited as retirement savings are reduced.

Things to consider:

Although it may seem logical to consider net worth, income may be a more accurate indicator as liquid assets and income would be needed to pay for long-term care expenses. Liquidating assets unexpectedly could be expensive and cumbersome.

OPTION #4 – MEDICARE

Medicare is a federal health insurance program for people who are either at least 65, living with disabilities, or have end-stage renal disease.

Advantage:

- Could pay up to 100 days of medically necessary care in a skilled nursing facility per benefit period. The first 20 days are paid 100%, assuming a 3-day prior hospitalization occurred.

Disadvantages:

- Days 21-100 require a co-payment.

- Medicare does not provide coverage for long-term care (custodial care).

- Benefits do not include care or assistance to help you remain in your home.

- Once Medicare stops paying, any Medicare supplemental insurance policy will also stop paying.

Things to consider:

Medicare pays for acute care (to get you back on your feet and on with life), but not for long-term care (custodial care) past 100 days per benefit period. Therefore, it is not a path for sustained long-term care coverage.

For additional details, visit www.medicare.gov.

OPTION #5 – MEDICAID

Medicaid is a jointly funded federal-state health insurance program for low-income and impoverished people. It covers children, the aged, the blind, disabled and other people who are eligible to receive federally assisted income-maintenance payments.

Advantage:

- For those with low income and limited resources, Medicaid would pay for nursing home care and in rare instances, some long-term care services at home or in the community.

Disadvantages:

- Medicaid sets limitations on the amount of assets you may own and the amount of income you may receive each month to remain eligible for benefits.

- Being dependent on Medicaid could limit your choices of care and facilities.

Things to consider:

Medicaid will pay for long-term care services if you have minimal assets and limited resources, but your choice of facilities will be limited.

For additional details, visit www.medicaid.gov.

OPTION #6 – TRADITIONAL LTC INSURANCE

Traditional long-term care insurance is the oldest form of comprehensive insurance that helps pay for the cost of long-term care expenses, including personal and custodial care in a variety of settings such as your home, a community organization, or other facility.

Advantages:

- Helps you maintain your independence should a long-term care need arise.

- Allows you to afford quality care.

- Reduces financial, emotional, and physical consequences that a long-term care need may cause to family members and loved ones.

- This type policy may qualify for the State Partnership Program, helping protect your assets that would otherwise need to be spent down prior to applying for Medicaid coverage, once your long-term care benefits have been exhausted.

- Dollar for dollar, this type of coverage gives you the most benefits of all options.

Disadvantages:

- You will go through full health underwriting.

- If approved, you'll pay significant ongoing monthly premiums.

- No premium guarantees, costs should rise in the future.

- If you don't file a claim, you won't get any paid premium returned to you.

- Uncertainty – can you afford to keep coverage years later when needed most?

Things to consider:

Traditional LTC insurance was the first type of LTC insurance offered over 30 years ago. Today, there are a multitude of LTC insurance solutions that are available because the insurance industry recognizes the current and future needs of the aging population. They've learned what consumers liked and didn't like about early traditional policies and designed much different and flexible LTC solutions.

Traditional long-term care type policies are the least sold today.[8]

---

8 Forbes, The Traditional Long-Term Care Insurance Market Crumbles, 9/8/17

OPTION #7 – SHORT-TERM CARE INSURANCE

Short-term care insurance works in the same way as traditional long-term care insurance, except the coverage is for a maximum of 365 days and is more affordable. There is no medical exam and only 7-10 questions to answer.

Advantages:

- No medical exams – gives someone with health problems an opportunity to secure LTC coverage

- Premiums are substantially less than a traditional LTC policy

Disadvantages:

- Maximum 365 days of coverage

- Some do not offer inflation protection

- Doesn't qualify for the State Partnership Program

Things to consider:

This is an option for those that have been declined in the past due to health problems or those that find traditional LTC premiums unaffordable.

OPTION #8 – ASSET-BASED LTC INSURANCE

Asset-based insurance could be a life insurance or annuity contract, with long-term care benefits. With this type of insurance policy, if some or all of the long-term care benefits are never used, then a death benefit would be paid to the beneficiary.

Advantages:

- Provides money for LTC needs, should they arise

- Alternative to self-funding, provides larger pool of money

- Provides money (death benefit) to your beneficiary upon death, if the policy has not been exhausted for long-term care expenses

- Premiums and benefits are guaranteed, eliminating future rate increases

Disadvantages:

- Does not qualify for the State Partnership Program

- Full underwriting required

- Will need to come up with a one-time single premium or pay over a limited period of years

Things to consider:

Asset-based plans make sense typically for those that have a chunk of money, say $50,000-$100,000 that they have tagged for future LTC expenses, currently in a CD, savings, or an underperforming account.

There are a couple of policies that offer a 10-pay premium instead of a lump-sum. This type of policy could triple or quadruple your premium for LTC purposes.

Disclosure for #8,#9 and #10: Life insurance is a financial product purchased first and foremost for the death benefit, but it may also offer riders and benefits that can assist with the cost of long-term care should the need arise. Life insurance policies are subject to medical underwriting, and in some cases, financial underwriting. Riders and life insurance products may not be available in all states and all claims are subject to the claims-paying ability of the insurer.

OPTION #9 – LIFE INSURANCE with a LONG-TERM CARE RIDER

A long-term care rider can be added to a life insurance policy at issue, to provide coverage for long-term care expenses that may arise.

Advantages:

- More comprehensive coverage than a chronic illness rider

- Premiums will not increase, and benefits will not change

- In addition to LTC protection, this policy provides a death benefit to your beneficiaries upon death if you don't use all of the LTC benefit

Disadvantages:

- Unlike traditional LTC insurance, premiums are not tax-deductible (businesses)

- Long-term care riders do not qualify for the State Partnership Program policy protection

- May not cover all long-term care costs

Things to consider:

This rider could make sense for those that need life insurance anyway. You could have your dollars perform double duty, access to cash to help pay for LTC expenses if needed, and if you never need extended care, then the death benefit will be paid to your beneficiary tax-free, if structured properly.

OPTION #10 – LIFE INSURANCE with a CHRONIC ILLNESS RIDER

A chronic illness rider can be purchased as optional protection on a life insurance contract. Chronic illness riders provide additional coverage should a chronic or non-recoverable illness occur.

Advantages:

- You have flexibility to use benefit payments however you choose, including home care.

- Benefits paid either to help with expenses for chronic illness, or to your beneficiaries as death benefit, or both.

Disadvantages:

- Additional premium requirements

- Generally, no inflation protection to help protect against rising health care costs

- May not cover all long-term care costs

- Benefits treated as accelerated life insurance death benefits, which reduces the remaining death benefit

Things to consider:

This rider could make sense for those that need life insurance anyway. You could have these dollars perform double duty, access to cash to help pay for LTC expenses if needed, and if you never need care, then the death benefit would be paid to your beneficiary tax-free, if structured properly.

Disclosure for #11 and #12: Annuities are insurance contracts designed for retirement or other long-term income needs. Some annuities offer riders and benefits that can assist with the cost of long-term care expenses.

OPTION #11 – ANNUITY with a LTC RIDER

A long-term care rider purchased as optional protection on an annuity contract. A rider fee will be deducted from your annuity's account value each year.

Advantages:

- Less-stringent medical underwriting than traditional long-term care insurance or life insurance would require

- Possible alternative to self-funding

Disadvantages:

- To receive benefits, you must first spend down your full annuity contract value first, then LTC benefits begin

- Withdrawals reduce the long-term care benefits and the death benefit

Things to consider:

An annuity is typically purchased to generate income either immediately or in the future. In recent years, more annuities have entered the marketplace with LTC riders as an option. These riders are not appropriate for everyone, but should be compared side by side with other LTC options.

OPTION #12 – ANNUITY INCOME DOUBLER

This is an option available on some fixed index annuity contracts. After a waiting period has been satisfied (typically 2 years), if the insured cannot perform 2 of 6 Activities of Daily Living, the income amount will double for up to 5 years for LTC purposes, then revert back to the original income amount for life. A typical rider fee would cost up to 1% per year.

Advantages:

- Minimal medical underwriting, just a few questions

- Lifetime income for two lives, if selected

Disadvantages:

- The doubled income payout may not cover all of your long-term care expenses

- Some policies only double if the insured is confined to a nursing home

- Typical two year waiting period before income doubler is active

Things to consider:

An annuity income doubler makes sense for those that are seeking guaranteed income as part of their overall retirement income plan. For a small annual fee, the insured would have the ability to double their income for LTC purposes, for up to 5 years.

OPTION #13 – REVERSE MORTGAGE

A reverse mortgage is an option for those age 62 and above with equity in their home. You could access these dollars to help pay for LTC expenses via a line of credit to be use as needed.

Advantages:

- No medical underwriting

- Access to your own money/equity

- No monthly premiums

Disadvantages:

- Ongoing fees and charges that build up annually that could become quite large, the longer the loan continues.

- You will have to continue paying property taxes and homeowners insurance.

- Waiting until you need LTC services to access home equity may only provide a portion of the care that you need.

Things to consider:

A reverse mortgage is another option to consider for LTC expenses. It's neither good or bad, your personal situation will dictate if it makes sense for you or not. For additional details, visit www.hud.gov

OPTION #14 – LIFE SETTLEMENT

For those fortunate enough to have an in-force life insurance policy, a life settlement could be a good source of funds to pay for long-term care expenses, if you find that the life insurance coverage is no longer needed.

A third-party would buy your policy and pay you a lump-sum amount. The third-party would pay all future premiums to keep the policy in-force, and become the beneficiary of your life policy.

Advantages:

- No underwriting
- Cash typically available in under 90 days

Disadvantages:

- The cash received may not cover all of your long-term care expenses

- Large fees to broker

- Could be considered taxable income

- Could disqualify you from Medicaid

Things to consider:

A life settlement could put some meaningful cash in your hands with no premium payments, but there are details to weigh before committing to this option.

So here we are, we have just covered the basics of 14 different ways that consumers could use to help protect themselves and their families from potential long-term care expenses.

Here are 3 questions that I believe you should be asking your financial advisor today;

1. What Plan Do We Have in Place for the Day that My, My Spouse, or My Partner's Health Fails?

2. What Will That Cost?

3. Where Will the Money Come from to Pay Those Bills?

To help you determine the best option for your personal situation, it is recommended that you have a discussion with a financial professional with expertise in long-term care planning. If you don't have one, ask your advisor to contact me and I'd be glad to help.

CHAPTER SIX

The State Long-Term Care Partnership Program

What Is It?

The State Long-Term Care Partnership Program is a federally-supported, state-operated initiative that allows individuals who purchase a qualified long-term care insurance policy to protect a portion of their assets that they would typically need to spend-down prior to qualifying for Medicaid coverage.

Once you purchase a Partnership policy and use some or all of the policy benefits, the amount of the policy benefits used will be disregarded for purposes of calculating eligibility for Medicaid; this means that you can keep assets up to the amount of the policy benefits that were paid under your policy.

History

The Long-Term Care Partnership Program originated in the late 1980's to address the increasing cost of state Medicaid expenditures for long-term care. It allowed individuals to purchase a long-term care insurance policy that protected an individual's assets up to a predetermined amount of policy benefits.

Benefits used would be disregarded when determining the individual's eligibility for state Medicaid. An amount equal to the benefits used would not have to be part of the asset spend-down for Medicaid eligibility.

During the late 1980's, only four states were able to implement a Partnership Program (California, Connecticut, Indiana, and New York) due to federal constraints. These four states are known as "grandfathered" Partnership states.

Effective February 8, 2006, the Federal Deficit Reduction Act of 2005 (DRA) allowed for the nationwide expansion of the Long-Term Care Insurance Partnership Program and asset protection on a dollar-for-dollar basis.

Each state can elect to implement a DRA Partnership Program for the citizens of that state. The DRA does not require states to participate. In turn, insurance companies need to decide if they will offer Partnership policies, and the policies must be certified as qualifying partnership policies.

The law specifies that anyone who purchases a tax-qualified long-term care insurance policy that meets stringent consumer protection standards and certain inflation requirements under the Partnership Program, would qualify for asset protection, on a dollar-for-dollar basis, up to the policy maximum.

It is important to note that the purchase of DRA Partnership coverage does not automatically qualify the coverage holder for Medicaid. In addition, all other Medicaid eligibility criteria and requirements will apply at the time an individual applies for Medicaid.

If you believe that you might have to rely on Medicaid for long-term care coverage, then a Partnership policy could save you a bunch of money.

You can visit the U.S. Department of Health and Human Services website at www.hhs.gov for the most up-to-date information on your state's participation.

CHAPTER SEVEN

Medicaid Planning

For years, Medicaid Planning has been a popular way for many Americans with sizable assets to plan for the eventuality that they will require long-term care.

For those unaware with the term, Medicaid Planning is the process by which those with the means to pay for their own long-term care divest themselves of their assets, down to the state required levels so that Medicaid (taxpayers/U.S. Treasury) will pay for their long-term care bills.

As a result, Medicaid Planning is a rather large industry with plenty of attorneys and financial services professionals helping clients try to shelter large piles of assets so that they can qualify for Medicaid.

Medicaid Planning Loopholes Closed

Medicaid Planning seemingly was working as advertised until February 8, 2006, when much of the wind was taken out of Medicaid Planners' sails.

It was on this date, that President George W. Bush signed into law the Deficit Reduction Act of 2005 (DRA), which eliminated many Medicaid Planning tactics. Not only did the DRA close the loopholes, it virtually eliminates the ability of someone with sizable assets to access governmental assistance.

Good News

There is a viable alternative for those with assets and one that the federal government has been supporting for years with deductions and tax-free benefits: the purchase of long-term care insurance.

For years, Congress has been indirectly informing America that the federal government cannot afford to meet the nation's long-term care needs. Let's review some of the legislative actions taken in recent years that affect Medicaid Planning.

It began with the Tax Equity and Financial Responsibility Act of 1982 instituting a 24 month look-back period for asset transfers prior to applying for Medicaid.

Then, the Medicare Catastrophic Coverage Act of 1988 extended the look-back period to 30 months.

The Omnibus Budget Reconciliation Act of 1993 extended it to 36 months.

The Deficit Reduction Act of 2005 (DRA) extended the look-back period to 60 months, where it stands as of 2018.

This pattern indicates that the U.S. government understands that it cannot afford to pay for the nation's long-term care needs and will continue to thwart efforts by anyone with assets, closing every loophole until there are none left.

As a result, long-term care insurance is the most viable course of action for individuals with assets to appropriately prepare for a potential long-term care need.

Here's a brief rundown on how the DRA now greatly reduces the viability of Medicaid Planning and emphasizes the importance of long-term care insurance as a planning option.

- **Change in the Look-Back Period for Asset Transfers**

  The DRA has gradually increased the look-back period to 60 months from its initial 24 months. If you gift or transfer any assets in the 60 months prior to applying for Medicaid, it would be determined that those assets could've been used to pay for your care and you would face a penalty.

  Penalty Example: Joe gives $100,000 cash to his daughter and one month later, he applies for Medicaid. The current cost of nursing home care where Joe lives is $10,000/month. Take the $100,000 gift and divide by the $10,000 monthly cost of care.

  $100,000 / $10,000 = 10 month penalty

  You would cover your care costs for 10 months before Medicaid would start paying.

- **Change in the Start of the Penalty Period**

  For any transfers during the look-back period, there is a penalty period that will begin from the first day the applicant enters the nursing home or otherwise becomes eligible for Medicaid. This means that full penalties will be imposed before Medicaid begins paying.

- **Notes, Loans, and Mortgages**

Under the DRA, any transfer of assets must be used to purchase a promissory note, loan or mortgage that has a repayment schedule that is actuarially sound, provides for equal payments with no deferral or balloon payments, and contains no cancellation at death provision.

- **Life Estates**

The DRA no longer permits the purchase of a life estate in another individual's home unless the applicant has legitimately lived in said home for at least one year prior to date of application for Medicaid.

- **Change in Treatment of Annuities**

Medicaid applicants must disclose any personal or spouse's interest in an annuity and the State must be named as the remainder beneficiary of the annuity as a condition of receiving Medicaid.

Failure to name the State as remainder beneficiary for at least the total amount of medical assistance paid on behalf of the annuitant, will result in the annuity being subject to transfer penalty rules. The State must also be named as a remainder beneficiary after the community spouse, minor child, or disabled child.

- **Substantial Home Equity**

Colorado applicants with home equity exceeding $572,000 will not be eligible for nursing home benefits. Each state has their own limit.

Through all these changes, Congress has stated loud and clear that Medicaid will provide funding for long-term care for only those who are truly indigent. Those individuals who have the means will be required to pay for their own long-term care expenses or purchase long-term care insurance.

Each state has their own rules, requirements and limitations on Medicaid eligibility. You could easily conduct an internet search for

Medicaid eligibility requirements for your home state.

As you know now, I live in the Denver, Colorado area, so here are the Medicaid eligibility requirements for Colorado:

Colorado Medicaid Long-Term Care Eligibility[9]

Colorado is an income-cap state, meaning that to be eligible for Medicaid long-term care benefits, there is an income limit. Non-income cap states allow applicants to spend-down money for their care, whereas income-cap states require the amount to be no higher than their limit at time of application.

Long-term care services can cover nursing home care or Home & Community-Based Services (HCBS). An individual receiving HCBS is not required to make a payment towards the cost of care.

Nursing home care provides 24-hour care in a professional setting, for help with basic activities and necessities. HCBS may take place in your home or a retirement community. HCBS can

9 www.colorado.gov/hcpf

include nurse assistance, home health aide, house cleaning, meal preparation or assistance with bathing and dressing.

Medicaid Eligibility[10]

- Eligibility is determined by an applicant's local county department of social services.

- Medicaid has both financial and medical related requirements.

- The income limit is up to 300% of the Social Security Income rate, adjusted annually. There is a personal needs allowance of $84.41 per month that is not factored into the countable income.

- The resource limit is $2,000 for individuals and $3,000 for couples both on Medicaid.

- Applicant must be 65 or older, or disabled, blind, or in a medical institution for at least 30 consecutive days (hospital and nursing facility), receiving a nursing facility level of care in the community for HCBS, or a combination of both.

10 www.colorado.gov/hcpf

- An individual receiving Medicaid LTC services in a long-term care facility is required to make a monthly payment towards the cost of care to the facility. The payment is based on gross monthly income with deductions.

Assets/Resources

Resources are divided into two categories: countable and exempt.

Countable resources include cash, checking accounts, savings accounts, CDs, mutual funds, IRAs, investment portfolios, bonds, and life insurance policies totaling more than $1,500, vehicles if more than one is owned, and properties.

Exempt resources include household goods, jewelry, one car, one home worth up to $572,000 (in Colorado), burial plots, life insurance policies if totaled less than $1,500. Limitations apply.

Annuity Rules

Usually, if an annuity is revocable and an individual can take a lump sum distribution, the annuity is a countable resource. If an annuity is assignable, it may be considered a transfer without fair consideration. If income is received from an annuity, it is considered income in the month it is received.

An annuity belonging to the community spouse (CS), which is irrevocable and non-assignable is not considered an available resource. An annuity belonging to the CS which is revocable is treated as an available resource, and the value of the annuity is included in the couple's total resources when determining the Community Spouse Resource allowance (CSRA).

The income a CS receives from an annuity is included in calculating the Community Spouse's Minimum Monthly Maintenance Needs Allowance (CSMMNA). Special Medicaid rules apply to couples to ensure that the CS who does not need LTC Services does not become impoverished when the other spouse needs Medicaid to help pay for the cost of LTC services.

The Medicaid applicant cannot give away their excess assets or sell anything below market value, as Medicaid reviews financial records as far back as 60 months prior to the application date.

Spousal Rules[11]

The community spouse (CS) can keep one-half of countable assets with a maximum value of $123,600. If the CS's assets do not equal $123,600, the CS is able to retain assets from the institutionalized spouse until the maximum is reached.

Community Spouse Impoverishment Protection

The CS can keep part of the institutionalized spouse's income if the CS has a monthly income of less than $2,030. The maximum amount of income that can be retained is $3,090, varying by case.

11 www.colorado.gov/hcpf

The HCBS and PACE Waiver Programs[12]

Medicaid can pay for care in the community – services at home, adult day care, and assisted living, under a federal waiver program for which states may apply called a Home & Community Based Services (HCBS) waiver.

For those 55 or older, there is the HCBS waiver program called Program of All Inclusive Care for the Elderly (PACE).

For a long-term care planning client with assets and income, PACE would not be a source to pay for care at home. Medicaid is a viable funding source for skilled nursing-home care.

If your goal is to remain in the community or at home, and you have significant assets and income, Medicaid is not a viable resource to pay for care.

CHAPTER EIGHT

Long-Term Care Insurance Tax Advantages

Individuals who purchase *tax qualified* long-term care insurance policies for themselves, their spouses, or their dependents, may claim the premiums paid as deductible personal medical expenses, but only if the individual itemizes his or her tax return.[13] There are very few individuals that will qualify to deduct their long-term care premiums paid.

More important than deductibility on the front-end, is the taxation of benefits received on the back-end (at time of utilization). Should the day come that you need to utilize the policy and benefits are paid to you, the benefits you receive are considered non-taxable income assuming you have a *tax qualified* policy.

13 Internal Revenue Code Sec. 213(a) and Sec. 213(d)(1)(D)

What is a Qualified Policy?

Almost all long-term care policies are considered *tax qualified* today.[14] The IRS states that a contract issued after 1996 is a qualified long-term care insurance contract if it meets the requirements of section 7702B, including the requirement that the insured must be a chronically ill individual.

A contract issued before 1997 is generally treated as a qualified long-term care insurance contract if it meets state law requirements for long-term care insurance contracts and it has not been materially changed.

To be qualified, a contract must adhere to all four of the following rules:

1. Be guaranteed renewable

2. Not provide for a cash surrender value or other money that can be paid, assigned, pledged, or borrowed

3. Provide that refunds, other than refunds on the death of the insured or complete surrender or cancellation of the contract,

14 www.irs.gov/pub/irs-pdf/i1099ltc.pdf

and dividends under the contract must be used only to reduce future premiums or increase future benefits

4. Generally not pay or reimburse expenses incurred for services or items that would be reimbursed under Medicare, except where Medicare is a secondary payer, or the contract makes per diem, or other periodic payments without regard to expenses

Qualified long-term care services

Qualified long-term care services are necessary diagnostic, preventive, therapeutic, curing, treating, mitigating, rehabilitative services, and maintenance and personal care services that are:

1. Required by a chronically ill individual

2. Provided pursuant to a plan of care prescribed by a licensed health care practitioner

Are Long-Term Care Insurance Benefits Taxable?

Individuals

Qualified long-term care benefits received by an individual are considered tax-free income. The insurance company that pays the benefits will issue an IRS 1099-LTC form indicating as much.

Long-Term Care State Tax Credit

Many states have a tax credit policy for those that purchase long-term care insurance.

In Colorado, it allows for a state income tax credit equal to the lesser of 25% of premiums paid or $150 per policy.[15]

The credit is available only to individual taxpayers with federal taxable income less than $50,000 (or 2 individuals filing jointly and claiming credit for one policy) and individuals filing jointly with $100,000 and claiming a credit for two policies. Unused credit may not be carried forward or refunded.

15 www.colorado.gov/pacific/sites/default/files/Income37.pdf

Businesses

Long-term care insurance offers significant tax breaks for businesses. Whether the founder of a large corporation or the owner of a smaller company, most business owners are interested in offering employees quality benefits at a reasonable price.

Tax advantages can also make certain benefits even more attractive – to both you and your employees. One often overlooked benefit, long-term care insurance can offer substantial tax breaks while allowing you to provide much-needed coverage to your employees.

Long-term care is needed when an individual has become incapacitated due to an accident or illness. Major medical insurance and Medicare weren't designed to cover these types of expenses. But most individuals never take time to determine how long-term care could factor into retirement.

Fortunately, many insurance companies are currently offering worksite long-term care insurance policies that are designed to be affordable for you and your employees. And, because most policies available today follow the guidelines set forth by the Health Insurance Portability and Accountability Act of 1996 (HIPAA), the premiums you pay are eligible for a tax deduction.

No matter what type of business you own, C-Corporation, S-Corporation, sole proprietorship, partnership or a Limited Liability Corporation, business contributions toward long-term care insurance premium payments on tax-qualified policies are fully deductible as a reasonable business expense, much like your premiums for major medical.

In addition, your employees receive policy benefits that are tax-free. In most situations, business premium contributions do not count as includable compensation for the employee.

Under HIPAA, long-term care insurance policies are portable and can be used as a carve-out benefit, meaning you can offer coverage to only your key employees if you so choose. The features available vary by policy, and it's important to shop around and consult with a specialist when selecting a worksite long-term care insurance product.

Depending on who you offer the coverage to, you might select a higher benefit level and shorter waiting period for key employees, and a more-affordable plan with a smaller benefit level and longer waiting period for the majority of your workforce.

You can even select a policy that can be paid-up in a certain amount of time, 10 years for instance, to encourage top staff members to stay with your company.

Whatever option you choose, the key is to offer quality and affordable coverage. Not only will you be working to attract and retain key employees, you're also enabling them to keep their independence as they age, by extending to them, the ability to choose for themselves where they will receive care.

Annuity Tax-Free Transfer

Another tax benefit from the tax-code is that you could transfer money tax-free from an annuity to cover premiums for a traditional long-term care policy or to pay for another annuity that provides long-term care benefits.

The transfer is known as a 1035 exchange (section 1035 of the tax code) and must be made directly from the annuity to pay the premiums. If you withdraw the money from the annuity rather than making the tax-free transfer, you'll owe income taxes on the gains, which are taxed first, before you recover your principal. Ask your long-term care professional for more information.

Life Insurance Tax-Free Transfer

You could also conduct a tax-free transfer from permanent life insurance, also called a 1035 exchange from a cash-value life insurance policy to pay long-term-care premiums, either for a traditional long-term care policy or a policy that combines life insurance and long-term care benefits.

The money could come from the policy's cash value, or you can use the policy's dividends to pay the long-term care premiums. This strategy can be useful as you get older and your primary needs change from life insurance to long-term care.

CHAPTER NINE

Selecting The Right Coverage

Long-term care insurance is evolving. There are many products available today that are based on innovative designs, all of which have the same purpose – to fund a plan to protect those whom the client cares about.

We refer to these products as long-term care insurance or extended-care solutions.[16] Generally, long-term care insurance policies come in three designs.

THREE DESIGNS

- Individual or 'traditional' long-term care insurance policy. Intended to cover just one person, but many policies offer a sharing provision and other couple's benefits if both spouses/partners apply.

16 CLTC Course 2018

- Linked-benefit policies (also called hybrid, combo, or asset-based). As their name implies, in linked-benefit policies, extended-care benefits are linked to another underlying product. That product can be either an annuity or life insurance.

- Life insurance that accelerates the death benefit to pay for extended care.

While it may seem that most policy provisions are set in stone and there's not much room for maneuvering, there are four major opportunities to tailor a policy, giving applicants control of designing a policy that best fit their needs.

Knowing how to finesse these four options could go a long way toward crafting a creative extended-care solution you're enthusiastic about.

FOUR FLEXIBLE BENEFITS[17]

Benefit Amount

Options include reimbursement policies and indemnity (per diem) policies.

---

17 CLTC Course 2018, www.longtermcare.acl.gov

A reimbursement policy, the most common type of benefit in traditional and linked-benefit policies, only pays based on covered, compensable expenses on extended care up to the daily or monthly benefit.

The operative word is 'compensable.' The caveat is that you should carefully review what services the carrier actually pays for. For example, one carrier might pay for an independent aide, while another requires services be provided through a professional agency.

An indemnity (or per diem) policy pays the full contract benefit, regardless of the actual expenses incurred. There are two types of indemnity benefits: cash and daily/professional.

Cash is more expensive. Daily /professional pays the fully-allowed daily amount for a compensable service, regardless of the cost.

For example, if you're monthly benefit is $4,000 and you only paid out $2,800 that month, you get to keep the remaining $1,200.

Benefit Period

This is the period of time that the benefit payments last after the payments begin. Common provisions range from one to six years, although some states require at least a two-year benefit period to be offered.

Most policies today employ a pool-of-benefits (also referred to as a pool-of-funds) approach in determining total plan benefits. The pool is determined simply by multiplying the daily benefit by 365 and the number of years selected in the policy.

Policies pay benefits from the pool in one of three ways: reimbursement, indemnity, or cash.

Inflation

The cost of professional care will increase over the years with inflation. Long-term care insurance offers several ways to plan for the rising cost of care.

Clients can pay-as-they-go with additional premium purchase options, or they can pay a higher planned premium and receive automatically-increased benefits over time. These inflation increases may range from a guaranteed 1% to 5% per year or they may track the Consumer Price Index (CPI), and the increases can be either compound or simple increases.

Elimination Period

An elimination period is sometimes called a waiting period. An elimination period is the period of time that must elapse after a benefit-triggering event has occurred, before benefits begin. Similar to an insurance policy's deductible, the elimination period is a means of controlling premium costs.

CHAPTER TEN

Long-Term Care Planning
Case Studies

In this chapter, I will introduce five hypothetical case studies that will give you an idea of the types of long-term care scenarios that unfold every day and possible strategies and solutions for those families.

These case studies are for educational purposes only and are not a recommendation for your particular situation.

SIX CASE STUDIES

#1 David & Carolyn, ages 58 and 54

David and Carolyn are successful business owners with no immediate plans to retire. They have two adult children and three young grandchildren.

Priorities

- Protect their assets from the expense of long-term care costs

- Provide an inheritance for family

- Would consider a retirement community when they are ready to downsize

Options to Consider

- Qualified traditional long-term care insurance plan for possible tax advantages as business owners

- Hybrid long-term care insurance plan to reposition assets not needed for retirement income to perform double duty – LTC and life insurance protection using same dollars

- Fixed annuity with an income doubler or LTC rider – generate income with LTC protection

- Refer to attorney for review of legal documents

- Life insurance review – seeking pennies to turn into dollars for heirs

#2 Shirley, age 58

Shirley lives with a partner and has no children. She is employed full time and coordinates care for her aging parents, who live in their own home.

Priorities

- Maintain her independence as she ages

- Stay in her home as long as possible

- Avoid a nursing home, just like her parents

Options to Consider

- Check with her employer about options for purchasing long-term care coverage through her job.

- Choose a Partnership-qualified traditional long-term care insurance policy that allows flexibility in her living options

- Consider annuities with long-term care benefits for retirement income

#3 Julie, age 61

Recently widowed, Julie lives with her son and his family. She works part-time and plans to continue working until age 70. Julie's mother, age 89, lives in a nearby Assisted Living Facility.

Priorities

- Enjoys living with her son and his family, but does not want to depend on them for daily care

Options to Consider

- Look into a Partnership-qualified long-term care policy that offers a cash option to pay family members for their care

- Consider a continuing care retirement community

#4 Steve & Patty, ages 55 and 53

Steve, works full-time and has type 2 diabetes that is controlled with diet and medication. Patty has always been an active volunteer and was the primary caregiver for her father, who had Alzheimer's and lived with them until his death.

Priorities

- Remain together and take care of one another as long as possible

- Would prefer to remain in their hometown, where they have many friends, rather than move out of state to be closer to their children.

Options to Consider

- Check with Steve's employer about purchasing a Partnership-qualified traditional long-term care insurance policy.

- Steve's diabetes and Patty's family history of Alzheimer's may make it difficult for them to qualify for long-term care coverage. They should consider a critical illness policy that includes benefits for Alzheimer's or a short-term care policy.

- Invest in fixed annuities that provide retirement income with an income doubler for LTC purposes, where there are just 1 or 2 health questions.

#5 Susan, age 60

Widowed with two adult children, Susan is employed full-time and plans to retire at age 65. She recently got a clean bill of health from her doctor, but has three siblings who are currently undergoing cancer treatment. She also has a life insurance policy.

Priorities

- Maintain autonomy over her living and health-care options

- Avoid nursing home care if possible

Options to Consider

- A Partnership-qualified traditional long-term care insurance policy

- Evaluate the merits of asset-based care versus a life settlement

- Consider a cancer policy due to the high family risk of cancer

- These case studies illustrate that everyone has their own set of circumstances and no outcome will be the same.

CHAPTER ELEVEN

Financial Consequences

Paying for care could disrupt every financial, tax, or legal plan that you have in place.[18] Paying for care causes a reallocation of resources, starting with income. The issue is that many successful retirees live on most of their income as they did during their working years. Shifting income to pay for care has a direct impact on the client's ability to keep financial commitments. These outcomes may include:

- Maintaining lifestyle expenses, including hobbies, travel, a boat, etc.

- Helping a child who has not made the best decisions in life

- Providing for a child or grandchild with special needs

18 Certified in Long-Term Care Course, 2018

- Helping pay for a grandchild's education

- Continuing obligations to a former spouse

- Gifting, tithing, or making charitable contributions

Although in theory, many of these expenses may be considered discretionary, in the world of a successful retiree, they are nondiscretionary. Asking income to pay for care and cover lifestyle expenses is, for practical purposes, double-counting it.

As a former wealth manager that served affluent clients, my former clients had sufficient assets to self-pay, but at what cost? Some would say, "if I ever need care, I've got enough assets."

I would then share the following:

Assets in a portfolio are really capital in nature, their purpose is not to be used to pay for care or any other expense in life, but to generate predictable streams of income that will keep up with a rising cost of living and that the client cannot outlive. The assets' job description is to generate income.

Using capital to pay for care creates unintended issues with:

- Unnecessary taxes

- Market timing

- Liquidity issues

- Leaving a legacy

And perhaps most importantly, every dollar used to pay for care is one dollar less available to generate income to keep future commitments.

For the less affluent, using assets to pay for care could start a financial death spiral. Assuming that the majority of assets are used to generate income, here is what could happen:

Year 1: The client tries to continue covering expenses with income generated by assets, while also paying for care from them. If care is paid from qualified or low cost-basis assets, a tax is incurred. The sale of assets is subject to market conditions, will it be up or down when you need to sell?

Year 2: Since there are now fewer assets to generate income, more assets have to be used to make up the difference. Of course, those assets are subject to the same taxes and market conditions. This is on top of the additional assets needed to pay for care.

Year 3: See year 2.

Year 4: See year 3.

In fact, this is exactly what clients are concerned about when they tell their financial advisors, "I want to avoid going into the principal."

Paying for extended care will likely force a reallocation of both income and assets. The problem is that none of the money was ever meant to pay for care, which means using it disrupts every plan you created to secure financial independence during retirement.

Typically, after each conversation, I hear "I never viewed it like that." Long-term care planning can help solve these issues.

CHAPTER TWELVE

Our 6-Step Process to Secure Long-Term Care Coverage

Long-term care coverage comes in many forms today and it is near impossible for the average consumer to vet the many options and different variations of those options when deciding on the best long-term care plan for you and your family.

Remember, you don't need long-term care coverage today, but when you need it, it most likely will be in 20-30 years. That is what you will want to solve for. What will it cost in 20, 25, or 30 years for long-term care services, and how will those bills get paid?

I recommend that you seek out a local long-term care specialist to guide you through a process, and at a minimum, that process should entail a full accounting of your personal financial picture, your family goals, your health history and what it is that you want to accomplish. From there, that process should analyze the information gathered, and research the various insurance and non-insurance ways that you could secure long-term care coverage. Then, I'll get back to you with the findings, so that an informed decision can be made on which option is most appropriate for you.

If you don't have a long-term care professional in your life that has a process to compare the 14 ways discussed in this book, I'd be honored to step in and fill that role.

My company, LTCi Solutions, LLC, offers consumers a complimentary PERSONAL LTC ASSESSMENT, which is a *6-Step Process* that compares the 14 insurance and non-insurance ways to secure long-term care coverage, and makes it easier for you to determine the best outcome that is most appropriate for your particular circumstances.

To request a PERSONAL LTC ASSESSMENT, visit www.ltcassessment.com

CHAPTER THIRTEEN

An Open Letter To CPAs, Attorneys, and Financial Advisors

After 20 years of business, in December 2016, I sold my comprehensive wealth management business to a larger firm. At that time, I was a fiduciary advisor, serving the affluent community in Houston, Texas. As a fiduciary advisor, it was my responsibility to design, implement, and monitor my clients' financial lives.

As a comprehensive wealth management firm, we addressed our clients' entire financial picture to include financial, insurance, tax, and legal issues.

Wealth management includes more than just taking capital and assets that were entrusted under our care and growing it so that income is available to pay for expenses later in life.

It involved financial, tax, insurance, and legal planning, or at the very least, a discussion on the issues.

Our firm worked collectively with our clients' other professionals, their CPAs, attorneys, and at times, their other financial advisors. It was a team approach, with each of us doing our part and working collectively for the best interest of the client.

If your clients don't have a plan in place for long-term care, that could absolutely disrupt your business model. My area of expertise is in a subject that has a direct impact on your business model and potentially has irreversible consequences to your clients' families.

Not having a plan for extended care could disrupt every tax plan, legal plan, or financial plan created for your clients, to minimize or eliminate taxes.

One goal of most tax and estate plans is to eliminate or minimize capital gain taxes at death, courtesy of the 'step-up' in basis rule.

Without a plan for long-term care, let's say your client had to liquidate assets to pay for care. When your client sell assets, they become subject to market timing. Sell in a down market and you lock in losses. Sell in an up market and you create an unnecessary tax bill. What's the answer?

There's no one size fits all answer, but I do know that tax-free is typically better than taxable, and long-term care benefits are paid as tax-free income.

NON-COMPETITOR SEEKING TO BE PART OF YOUR TEAM: As you know, I sold my comprehensive wealth management firm in December 2016 to a larger firm and relocated to Colorado.

After a one-year sabbatical, I started a new company, LTCi Solutions, LLC that focuses exclusively on long-term care education, planning, and solutions, for those age 50 and better.

MY OFFER: Please think about having this conversation with your client. If you prefer, I could have that conversation for you as the expert you bring to the table.

I would ask the right questions to design a plan so that your clients can confidently keep their commitments, and your business model doesn't get disrupted.

HELPFUL RESOURCES

Here are some of my favorite sources that have additional information and resources for those that are planning for long-term care.

Alzheimer's Association – www.alz.org

American Association of Long-Term Care Insurance – www.aaltci.org
A national long-term care insurance trade association. Excellent consumer information on long-term care insurance.

A Place For Mom – www.aplaceformom.com
Assists seniors in relocating to a senior community, assisted living or memory care facility, or apartment in their area.

Caregiver – www.caregiver.com A virtual supermarket of resources for caregivers.

Colorado Insurance Department – www.colorado.gov
Colorado State Partnership Program FAQs.

Genworth's Cost of Care Calculator – www.genworth.com
Local average pricing of long-term care costs all over America. Input your city to see your costs today.

Long-Term Care Shoppers Guide – www.naic.org
Informative booklet on the ins and outs of long-term care insurance.

National Alliance for Caregiving – www.caregiving.org
All about supporting caregivers.

Medicare – www.medicare.gov

Medicaid – www.medicaid.gov
Home & Community Based Services provided by Medicaid.

National Association of Geriatric Care Managers – www.caremanager.org
Teaches you about aging well and what geriatric care managers do.

Real Life Stories – www.lifehappens.org
Powerful, moving videos showing and
describing people who benefited from owning
long-term care insurance.

Senior Advisor – www.senioradvisor.com
Similar to tripadvisor.com, except that it is for
rating, finding, and reviewing assisted living, and
nursing facilities.

U.S. Dept. of Health & Human Services –
www.longtermcare.acl.gov
Resources and weblinks to other long-term care
sources.

CPSIA information can be obtained
at www.ICGtesting.com
Printed in the USA
FFHW011930291218
50017426-54774FF